W9-BXW-241

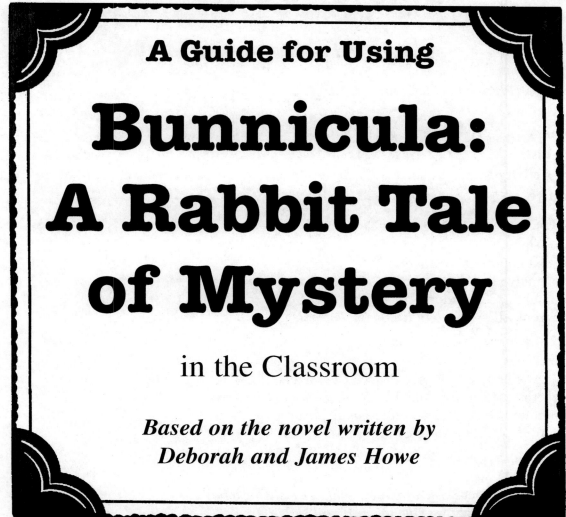

A Guide for Using

Bunnicula: A Rabbit Tale of Mystery

in the Classroom

Based on the novel written by Deborah and James Howe

*This guide written by **Amy Shore***

Teacher Created Materials, Inc.
6421 Industry Way
Westminster, CA 92683
www.teachercreated.com
©*1995 Teacher Created Materials*
Reprinted, 2003
Made in U.S.A.
ISBN 1-55734-534-1

Edited by
Stephanie Buehler, M.P.W., M.A.
Illustrated by
Kathy Bruce
Cover Art by
Wendy Chang

Table of Contents

- ◆ Quiz Time!
- ◆ Hands-On Project—*Nutrition*
- ◆ Cooperative Learning Activity—*Doing the Bunny Hop!*
- ◆ Curriculum Connection—*Social Studies: Does Transylvania Exist?*
- ◆ Into Your Life—*Reading Response Journals*

- ◆ Quiz Time!
- ◆ Hands-On Project—*Papier–Mâché Characters*
- ◆ Cooperative Learning Activity—*Action Verbs Brainstorm*
- ◆ Curriculum Connections—*Art: Family Portrait*
- ◆ Into Your Life—*Reading Other Scary Stories*

- ◆ Quiz Time!
- ◆ Hands-On Project—*The Monroe Family's Pets' Cookbook*
- ◆ Cooperative Learning—*Bunnicula Board Game*
- ◆ Curriculum Connection—*Math: Dining at the Bunny Cafe*
- ◆ Into Your Life—*What Are You Afraid Of?*

- ◆ Quiz Time!
- ◆ Hands-on Project—*Bunnicula TV Show*
- ◆ Cooperative Learning Activity—*Monsters*
- ◆ Curriculum Connection—*Science: Researching Bats*
- ◆ Into Your Life—*A Family Mystery*

After the Book *(Post-reading Activities)*

Introduction

A good book can touch our lives like a good friend. Within its pages are words and characters that can inspire us to achieve our highest ideals. We can turn to it for companionship, recreation, comfort, and guidance. It also gives us a cherished story to hold in our hearts forever.

In Literature Units, great care has been take to select books that are sure to become good friends.

Teachers who use this literature unit will find the following features to supplement their own valuable ideas.

- Sample Lesson Plans

- Pre-reading Activities

- A Biographical Sketch and Picture of the Author

- A Book Summary

- Vocabulary Lists and Suggested Vocabulary Activities

- Chapters grouped for study, with each section including:
  - *quizzes*
  - *hands-on projects*
  - *cooperative learning activities*
  - *cross-curriculum connections*
  - *extensions into the reader's own life*

- Post-reading Activities

- Book Report Ideas

- Research Ideas

- Culminating Activities

- Three Different Options for Unit Tests

- Bibliography

- Answer Key

We are confident that this unit will be a valuable addition to your planning and hope that as you use our ideas, your students will increase the circle of "friends" that they can have in books.

Sample Lesson Plan

Each of the lessons suggested below can take from one to several days to complete.

LESSON 1

- Introduce and complete some or all of the pre-reading activities found on page 5.
- Read "About the Authors" with your students. (page 6)
- Read the "Book Summary" for your own information. (page 7)
- Introduce the vocabulary list for Section 1. (page 8) Ask students for possible definitions.

LESSON 2

- Read Chapters 1 and 2. Place vocabulary words in context and discuss their meanings.
- Go over the "Word Detective" worksheet and discuss the meanings of the words. (page 10)
- Choose a vocabulary activity. (page 9)
- Discuss Harold's diet and complete the activity on nutritious snack foods. (page 12)
- Learn the Bunny Hop dance. (page 13)
- Discuss the geographical setting of the legend behind the story. (page 14)
- Begin the reading response journals. (page 15)
- Administer the Section 1 quiz. (page 11)
- Introduce the vocabulary list for Section 2. (page 8) Ask students for possible definitions.

LESSON 3

- Read Chapters 3 and 4. Place vocabulary words in context and discuss their meanings.
- Choose a vocabulary activity. (page 9)
- Discuss the characters of Harold, Chester, and Bunnicula and make papier-mâché representations. (page 17)
- Brainstorm action verbs. (page 18)
- Draw a family portrait. (page 19)
- Choose a different scary book and write a report. (page 20)
- Administer the Section 2 quiz. (page 16)
- Introduce the vocabulary list for Section 3. (page 8) Ask students for possible definitions.

LESSON 4

- Read Chapters 5 and 6. Place vocabulary words in context and discuss their meanings.
- Choose a vocabulary activity. (page 9)
- Prepare recipes. (pages 22–23)
- Play "Bunnicula Board Game." (pages 24–26)
- Solve math problems based on a menu. (pages 27–28)
- Discuss and write about real and imagined fears. (page 29)
- Administer the Section 3 quiz. (page 21)
- Introduce vocabulary list for Section 4. (page 8) Ask students for possible definitions.

LESSON 5

- Read Chapters 7 through 9. Place vocabulary words in context and discuss their meanings.
- Choose a vocabulary activity. (page 9)
- Discuss scenes and prepare scroll for TV show. (page 31)
- Discuss and write about monsters. (page 32)
- Discuss and research bats. (page 33)
- Discuss mysteries and clues. (page 34)
- Administer the Section 4 quiz. (page 30)

LESSON 6

- Discuss any questions your students may have about the book. (page 35)
- Assign book reports, writing ideas, and research ideas. (pages 36–38)
- Begin working on culminating activity. (pages 39–40)

LESSON 7

- Complete and present culminating activity.
- Administer unit tests 1, 2, and/or 3. (pages 41–43)
- Discuss the test answers and other possibilities.
- Discuss the students' enjoyment of the book.
- Provide a list of related reading for your students. (page 44)

Before the Book

Build background knowledge by introducing the following information to students.

Dracula

Dracula is a novel written by English author Bram Stoker and published in 1897. In this frightening story, the main character is a terrible nobleman, Count Dracula, of Transylvania, a region of Romania. Dracula is a vampire—a corpse that comes to life at night, attacks people, and sucks their blood. Dracula is stopped when two men track him down and destroy him by driving a stake through his heart. The story is probably best known as a motion picture, *Dracula*, produced in 1931 and again in 1994.

Before you begin reading *Bunnicula* with your students, do some pre-reading activities to stimulate interest and enhance comprehension. Here are some activities that might work well in your class.

1. Predict what the story might be about by hearing the title.

2. Predict what the story might be about by looking at the cover illustration.

3. Discuss other books James Howe has written that the students might have read. (examples: *Howliday Inn, The Celery Stalks at Midnight*)

4. Answer these questions:

   Are you interested in:
   — *a story about a dog who becomes a hero?*
   — *a story with mysterious clues?*
   — *a story about jealousy over a newcomer in the house?*

5. Work in groups to create scary stories. Present the stories in class, perhaps dramatizing them with props or narration.

6. Use the picture on page 48 to help introduce *Bunnicula* to your class. The picture can also be used as a cover for response journals or the centerpiece of a bulletin board display of student work.

About the Authors

Bunnicula was written by husband-and-wife team Deborah and James Howe. Deborah Howe was born in Boston, Massachusetts, on August 12, 1946. She attended Boston University and received her B.F.A. in 1968. Before writing *Bunnicula* with her husband, she worked for nearly a decade as an actress in New York.

James Howe was born August 2, 1946, in Oneida, New York. Like Deborah, he also received his B.F.A. from Boston University in 1968 and an M.A. from Hunter College in 1977. One day, he hit on the idea of a "vampire bunny," but it was Mrs. Howe who decided that *Bunnicula: A Rabbit Tale of Mystery* should become a children's book and that they should work together. Mr. Howe describes the process:

> *We sat around our kitchen table one night throwing ideas out to each other. It was in this session we decided Bunnicula's victims would be vegetables, not people. It was truly a collaborative process. One of us would talk out loud while the other wrote frantically. As we inspired each other's thinking, the ideas and words overlapped, until there were sentences, phrases, even, that were truly the creation of two people.*

Sadly, Mrs. Howe battled cancer and died in 1978. The team's second book, *Teddy Bear's Scrapbook*, was published in 1980, after her death. Mr. Howe later married Betsy Imershein, a theater producer. He continues to write children's books, finding the activity to have "a kind of creative control that is deeply fulfilling," though he does not believe he was born to write:

> *Writing, at least professionally, is a recent development. But the creative itch has been with me for as long as I can remember. And it has always been strong enough that it demanded to be scratched.*

Bunnicula: A Rabbit-Tale of Mystery

by Deborah and James Howe

(Avon Camelot Books, 1979)

(Available in Canada, UK, and Australia from International Book Dist. Contact Al Polan 201-967-5810)

The Monroe family's intellectual pet cat, Chester, turns detective when the family brings home a rabbit abandoned in a nearby theater seat, found when they go to a showing of *Dracula*. While Harold, the family dog, is disappointed in Bunnicula's inability to play, Chester notices very different things. For example, Chester decides the rabbit's teeth look very much like fangs and its fur looks very much like Dracula's cape.

Certain that the Monroes have a vampire bunny on their hands, Chester unsuccessfully tries to convince Harold that they need to get rid of Bunnicula. When vegetables from the refrigerator show up white (and, with closer examination, fang holes are found by Chester) and Bunnicula keeps waking at midnight to go into the kitchen, Chester does his best vampire imitation to show the Monroes what a mistake they have made. When the Monroes fail to understand Chester's message, Chester decides it is up to him to protect the family from Bunnicula, even resorting to garlic to ward off the rabbit. Soon, Bunnicula is so frightened of Chester that he will not leave his cage, becoming weak and hungry.

Fortunately, Harold tries to save the day by getting Bunnicula to a bowl of salad on the family dining table. Although Harold's plan is foiled, the Monroes finally get the idea that Bunnicula is both starving and scared. All three pets are taken to the vet, where Bunnicula is prescribed a liquid diet, Harold finds out he does not need shots after all, and Chester, diagnosed with a case of sibling rivalry, is sent to meet a pet psychiatrist.

Vocabulary Lists

On this page are vocabulary lists which correspond to each sectional grouping of chapters. Vocabulary activity ideas can be found on page 9. Vocabulary knowledge may be evaluated by including selected words in the quizzes and tests. This can be done with multiple choice, matching, or fill-in-the-blank questions.

Section 1
(Chapters 1–2)

admiration	vivid
reverie	eerie
tranquil	gypsy
decipher	hideous
compromise	fangs

Section 2
(Chapters 3–4)

analysis	sauntered
indulgent	scornfully
romp	dialect
pendulum	vampire
subtle	zucchini

Section 3
(Chapters 5–6)

panic	emanated
seized	pendant
throttle	immobile
blight	stake
organic	pathetic

Section 4
(Chapters 7–9)

exemplary	nourishment
distressed	reluctance
listless	overwrought
disaster	psychiatrist
petrified	narrative

Vocabulary Activities

You can help your students learn and retain the vocabulary in *Bunnicula* by providing them with interesting vocabulary activities. Here are a few ideas to try.

 As a group activity, have students work together to create an **illustrated dictionary** of the vocabulary words.

Play vocabulary concentration. The goal of this game is to match vocabulary words with their definitions. Divide the class into groups of two to five students. Have the students make two sets of cards the same size and color. On one set have them write the vocabulary words, on the second set have them write the definitions. All cards are mixed together and placed face down on the table. A player picks two cards. If the pair matches the word with its definition, the player keeps the cards and takes another turn. If the cards do not match, they are returned to their places face down on the table, and another player takes a turn. Players must concentrate to remember the locations of the words and their definitions. The game continues until all matches have been made. This is an ideal activity for free exploration time.

Play vocabulary charades. In this game, vocabulary words are acted out.

Play vocabulary mum ball. One student says a vocabulary word before throwing a ball made of soft material to another student. The catcher must define the word to stay in the game. If the catcher cannot define the word or drops the ball, he or she is out of the game.

Keep a word wall in your room. When students find a new vocabulary word in their reading, have them write the new word, its definition, and a sentence using the word on an index card and staple it to a bulletin board set aside for this purpose.

Play bingo with vocabulary words. Hand out worksheets with an empty grid on which students will write a different vocabulary word in each square. As you or a student volunteer calls out a vocabulary word, students cover it with a marker if it appears on their grid. Continue playing until a student has filled the grid with markers straight across, down, or diagonally. The student who has bingo must then define each word along the line before being declared the winner.

Challenge students to find **synonyms** or **antonyms** for the vocabulary words from within the story.

You probably have more ideas to add to this list. Try them. See if experiencing vocabulary on a personal level increases your students' vocabulary interest and retention.

Word Detective

For each vocabulary word, first hunt through the section in the book for the word and copy the sentence in which you find it. Second, rewrite the sentence, using a synonym or phrase that would make sense and keep the same meaning.

Words   Sentences

Words	Sentences
	1. _____ _____ 2. _____ _____
	1. _____ _____ 2. _____ _____
	1. _____ _____ 2. _____ _____
	1. _____ _____ 2. _____ _____
	1. _____ _____ 2. _____ _____

Quiz Time!

Answer the following questions about Chapters 1 and 2.

1. Where did the Monroes find the bunny? What effect did this have on Chester's imagination?

   _____

2. Describe the bunny's unusual appearance. _____

   _____

3. List some of the names the family suggested for their new pet._____

   _____

4. How did the Monroes come up with the name "Bunnicula"?_____

   _____

5. What did you learn about Harold's family background? _____

   _____

6. Chester is not your typical cat. What were some things that made him different? _____

   _____

7. Toby and Peter argued over who gets to keep which pet in their rooms. Who had the better reason to keep Bunnicula? Why? _____

   _____

8. What incident in Chapter 2 suggested that Chester had an active imagination? _____

   _____

9. Why do you think Chester was afraid of Bunnicula? _____

   _____

10. On the back of this paper, draw two pictures of Bunnicula, one as he really is and one as Chester sees him. Then state below the reason you think Chester sees Bunnicula this way.

    _____

    _____

    _____

    _____

    _____

    _____

    _____

    _____

    _____

Nutrition

Members of the Monroe household have their own particular likes and dislikes when it comes to food. Of course, some foods are more nutritious than others. A peanut butter sandwich contains protein, but a green sourball basically contains only sugar.

A balanced diet contains a variety of foods needed for the body to function and even allows for occasional treats. The U.S. Department of Agriculture revised the dietary guidelines for good nutrition in 1992. A pyramid shape was chosen to show that carbohydrates (bread, cereal, rice, and pasta) form the basis of a good diet, with other foods shown in decreasing, but necessary, quantities.

In a small group of three to four students, you will create a balanced diet for a day by following the food pyramid guidelines. Once you have your day planned, write in the items in the pyramid below. Be sure to include healthy snacks to round out your meals.

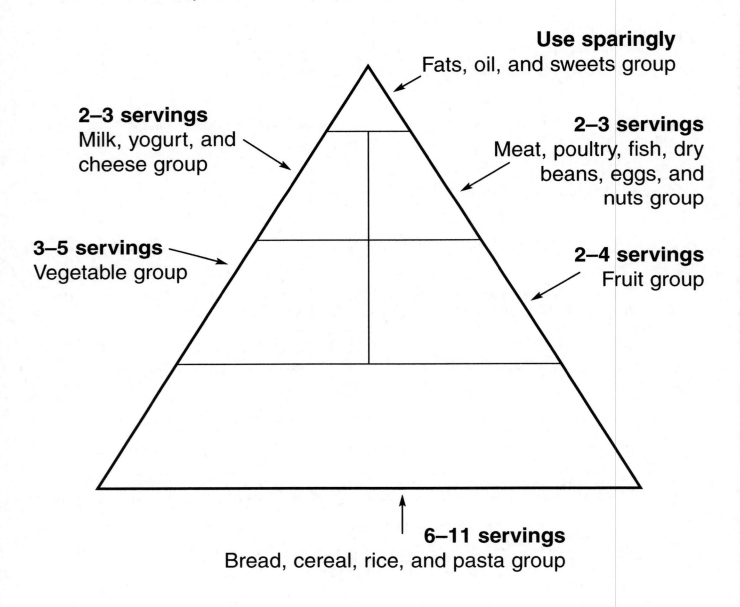

Use sparingly
Fats, oil, and sweets group

2–3 servings
Milk, yogurt, and cheese group

2–3 servings
Meat, poultry, fish, dry beans, eggs, and nuts group

3–5 servings
Vegetable group

2–4 servings
Fruit group

6–11 servings
Bread, cereal, rice, and pasta group

Doing the Bunny Hop!

The Bunny Hop was created during the Big Band era of the thirties. The dance is still enjoyed today since the steps are fun and so easy that everyone can join in.

How to do the Bunny Hop:

1. Have the students line up and turn their heads to watch the instructor.

2. Demonstrate the steps.

   a. Put the right foot out twice with the heel down and toe up.

   b. Repeat twice with left foot.

   c. Next, take a small hop forward and a small hop back.

   d. Finally, hop forward three times.

3. After the students have mastered these steps, have them each place their hands on the waist or shoulder of the person in front of them and try the dance with music.

Check your local library for the recording of "The Bunny Hop" by Ray Anthony and Leonard Auletti (Capitol Records No. 2251).

Does Transylvania Exist?

When Bunnicula is found, there is a note with him written in a rare language from the region of the Carpathian mountains, or Transylvania. Is there really a Transylvania, and if so, where can it be found? Find out more about Transylvania by answering the questions below, using an encyclopedia and other reference books.

1. Where is Transylvania located? _____

2. Name the countries adjacent to this region. _____

   _____

3. What is the climate in Transylvania? _____

4. List four major geographical features found in this region. _____

   _____

5. List four natural resources found in this region. _____

   _____

6. What language is spoken in Transylvania? _____

7. Label the region of Transylvania on the map of Romania below. Write in the names of geographical features and show the location of the region's largest city.

ROMANIA

Bucharest ●

8. How does your knowledge of Transylvania change your ideas about *Bunnicula?*

   _____

   _____

9. Why do you think the author of *Dracula* chose Transylvania as a setting for his story?

   _____

   _____

Reading Response Journals

One great way to insure that the reading of *Bunnicula* becomes a personal experience for each student is to include the use of reading response journals in your plans. In these journals, students can be encouraged to respond to the story in a number of ways. Here are a few ideas.

Tell students that the purpose of the journal is to record their thoughts, ideas, observations, and questions as they read *Bunnicula*.

Provide students with, or ask them to suggest, topics from the story that would stimulate writing. Here are a few examples from the chapters in Section 1:

How does Chester react to another pet in the house? What does he do to show his feelings?

Do you think Chester will discover that Bunnicula is a vampire?

What is the relationship between the two brothers? Do the pets act like them in any way?

After the reading of each chapter, students can write one or more new things they learned in the chapter.

Ask students to draw their responses to certain events or characters in the story, using the blank pages in their journals.

Tell students that they may use their journals to record diary-type responses.

Encourage students to bring their journal ideas to life. Ideas generated from their journal writing can be used to create plays, debates, stories, songs, and art displays.

Give students quotes from the novel and ask them to write their own responses. Be sure to do this before you go over the quotations in class. In groups, they could list the different ways students might respond to the same quote.

Allow students time to write in their journals daily. Explain to the students that their reading response journals can be evaluated in a number of ways. Here are a few ideas.

Personal reflections will be read by the teacher, but no corrections or letter grades will be assigned. Credit is given for effort, and all students who sincerely try will be awarded credit.

Teacher Note: If a grade is desired for this type of entry, you may grade according to the number of journal entries completed. For example, if five journal assignments were made and a student conscientiously completes all five, then he or she receives an "A."

Nonjudgmental teacher responses should be made as you read journals to let the students know you are reading and enjoying their journals. Here are some types of responses that will please your journal writers and encourage them to write more.

"You have really found what's important in the story!"

"You write so clearly, I almost feel as if I am there."

"If you feel comfortable, I'd like you to share this with the class. I think they'll enjoy it as much as I have."

Quiz Time!

Answer the following questions about Chapters 3 and 4.

1. Name three things that Harold noticed Bunnicula could not do:

   a. _____

   b. _____

   c. _____

2. What did Harold like to eat? What did he hate?

   _____

   _____

3. What did Bunnicula do in the Monroes' house after midnight?

   _____

   _____

4. Tell about the strange object that Mr. Monroe found in the refrigerator.

   _____

   _____

5. What did Chester think caused the strange object to change color?

   _____

6. What clues did Chester use from *Mark of the Vampire* to convince Harold that Bunnicula was a vampire bunny?

   _____

7. Which pet is smarter, Harold or Chester? Why?

   _____

   _____

8. What caused Harold and Chester to investigate the kitchen, and what did they find?

   _____

   _____

9. What brave thing did Harold do?

   _____

10. How do you think Bunnicula opened the refrigerator?

    _____

    _____

    _____

Creating Papier-Mâché Characters

The art of papier-mâché turns old newspaper and starch or glue into sculpture. Begin collecting old newspapers and cardboard tubes such as those found inside paper towels; you will probably need about two newspapers and one tube per student. Work out an equitable way for one-third of your students to make Bunnicula; one-third, Chester; and one-third, Harold, such as drawing the characters' names from a hat.

Materials:

- old newspapers
- masking tape
- water
- cardboard tubes
- liquid starch or white glue
- bowls or other containers for liquid mixture

Directions:

1. Crush several large sheets of newspaper together to form a large ball for the body and a small ball for the head of each character.
2. Use masking tape to secure the head to the body. You may also wish to use a few strips of masking tape to help hold together the shape of the newspaper balls.
3. Cut cardboard tubes as shown and tape to the front of the character's body to create legs.
4. Use newspaper to create other features such as a tail and ears, taping them to the character as well.

5. Pour about one cup (250 mL) of liquid starch or white glue into bowl or container and add enough water to make a mixture the consistency of shampoo.
6. Tear more newspaper into manageable strips. Dip the newspaper into the liquid mixture, using your fingers to wipe any excess liquid back into the bowl.
7. Apply the wet newspaper evenly to the character's form, creating a single, smooth layer. Allow to dry overnight.
8. Repeat with a second application of wet newspaper strips. Allow to dry at least overnight.
9. Use tempera paints to create the character's features such as eyes, nose, fur, etc.
10. Make a display of the characters. For fun, you may want to give out a variety of awards such as "Most Expressive Face," "Neatest," etc. You may also wish to invite students from other classrooms to see your creations.

Action Verbs Brainstorm

Bunnicula opens on a rainy night, but a "brainstorm" is a very different type of storm. In a brainstorm, people work together to come up with many different thoughts or ideas. Work with a partner to come up with as many action verbs as you can that fit Bunnicula, Harold, and Chester. For example, action words for Bunnicula might include "eats" and "escapes." When you finish, use five of your favorite verbs from each list to write sentences about that character.

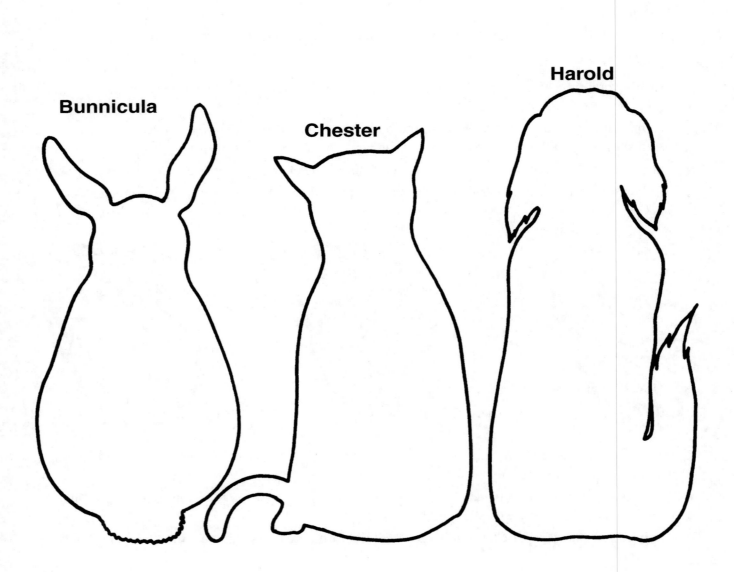

Family Portrait

Draw a picture with your crayons of what the Monroe family looks like with their pets. Be sure to put them in an appropriate room of the house, such as the living room or kitchen. You may wish to show each family member holding something typical, such as showing Toby with cupcakes.

Reading Other Scary Stories

In Chapters 3 and 4 of *Bunnicula*, Chester observes many scary details about Bunnicula, such as his odd fur markings, glistening fangs, peculiar sleeping habits, and the mysterious occurrence of white vegetables. All these clues both excite the reader and frighten Chester into believing Bunnicula is a real vampire.

Select and read another scary book by James Howe or a different author, then answer the questions below.

1. Who is the author and what is the book title?_____

2. Does the book title give any clues?_____

3. What was the most frightening person, creature, or event in the book?

    _____

    _____

4. How did the characters in the book react to the frightening occurrence?

    _____

    _____

5. What role did the setting of the book play in the story?

    _____

6. Who was the hero and who was the villain in the story? _____

7. At what point in the book did the story become frightening?

    _____

8. At what point in the book did you know everything would turn out all right?

    _____

9. What were some details the author included to create suspense?

    _____

    _____

10. Why do you think people enjoy reading scary stories?

    _____

    _____

    _____

    _____

Quiz Time!

Answer the questions for Chapters 5 and 6.

1. What did Mrs. Monroe and her family find next in the kitchen?

   _____

2. What did Peter think caused the vegetables to change, and what was his solution?

   _____

3. Name two things Chester did to show the Monroes that he thought Bunnicula was a vampire.

   _____

4. What happened to Chester after the Monroes watched him?

   _____

   _____

5. Describe the article of clothing Chester wore and tell how Chester felt about wearing it.

   _____

   _____

6. What awful odor did Harold smell, and why was it in the air?

   _____

   _____

7. What happened to Chester when the Monroes got a whiff of him?

   _____

   _____

8. Why did Harold have such a hard time getting Bunnicula out of his cage?

   _____

   _____

9. Why did Chester try using a "steak" to kill Bunnicula? What should he have been using instead?

   _____

   _____

10. Where does Chester end up after the steak incident? How does Harold feel about Chester's predicament?

   _____

   _____

The Monroe Family's Pets' Cookbook

Food is a central topic of interest in *Bunnicula.* Cut and assemble the recipe book, create a cover, then try the recipes together in class.

- -

Bunnicula's Vitamin-Rich Carrot Squares
(makes 24 small squares)

Ingredients:

2 c. (480 mL) sugar

1½ c. (360 mL) salad oil

2 c. (480 mL) grated carrots

1 t. (5 mL) vanilla

4 eggs

3 c. (720 mL) self-rising flour, sifted

1 c. (240 mL) pecans, chopped

Have ready:

a greased 9" x 11" (23 cm x 28 cm) pan

Procedure:

1. Preheat oven to 300°F (154° C).
2. Using an electric mixer and adding eggs one at a time, cream together sugar and eggs in a medium bowl.
3. Gradually add oil and sifted flour.
4. Using a spoon, add grated carrots, pecans, and vanilla and blend thoroughly.
5. Pour into prepared oblong pan.
6. Bake 1 hour and 10 minutes or until knife blade inserted for testing comes out clean.

- -

Mrs. Monroe's Healthful Salad

Ingredients:

2 heads green cabbage, shredded

½ head purple cabbage, shredded

6 radishes, sliced thin

2 carrots, grated

½ cup (120 mL) shelled sunflower seeds

½ cup (120 mL) golden raisins

1 bottle cole slaw dressing

Procedure:

1. Prepare all ingredients and place in a large salad bowl.
2. Add bottled cole slaw dressing to moisten ingredients and toss.

- -

The Monroe's Family's Pets' Cookbook *(cont.)*

- -

Harold's "It's No Mystery" Microwave Chocolate Fudge
(makes 64 pieces)

Ingredients:

1 lb. (453.6 g) confectioner's sugar   ½ c. (120 mL) cocoa powder

¼ c. (60 mL) milk   1 t. (5 mL) vanilla

½ c. (120 mL) margarine, sliced for easier melting

Have ready:

a greased 8" x 8" (20 cm x 20 cm) pan

Procedure:

1. Mix sugar and cocoa powder in a medium-sized, microwave-proof bowl.
2. Add milk and margarine to the dry ingredients.
3. Microwave together for 2 minutes on high.
4. Stir in vanilla and microwave briefly to melt any solid margarine.
5. Pour into prepared pan and either freeze for 20 minutes or refrigerate for 1 hour.
6. Cut into 1" (2.54 cm) squares to serve and watch it disappear.

- -

Chester's Whiff-of-Garlic Bread

Ingredients:

½ stick (60 mL) of butter or margarine
3–4 large cloves of garlic, finely minced
1 large loaf of unsliced crusty bread

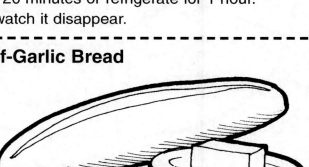

Have ready:

foil for wrapping loaves

Procedure:

1. Preheat oven to 300° F (154° C).
2. Prepare the loaf by slicing in half horizontally, then slicing vertically about 2" (5 cm) apart, taking care not to cut through the crust.
3. In a small, microwave-proof bowl, melt butter or margarine for 45 seconds on high. Continue to microwave for 10 seconds at a time until butter or margarine completely melts.
4. Stir minced garlic into butter or margarine.
5. Use a basting brush or rubber spatula to spread the garlic mixture over the bread.
6. Wrap bread in foil and heat in oven until warm, about 15 minutes. To serve, open foil and pull slices apart.

- -

Bunnicula Board Game

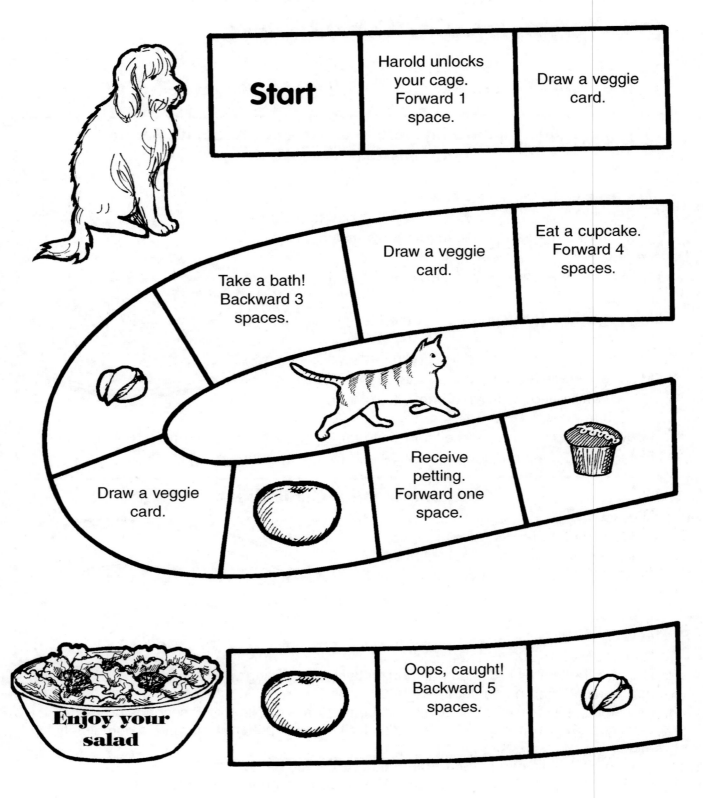

Bunnicula Board Game *(cont.)*

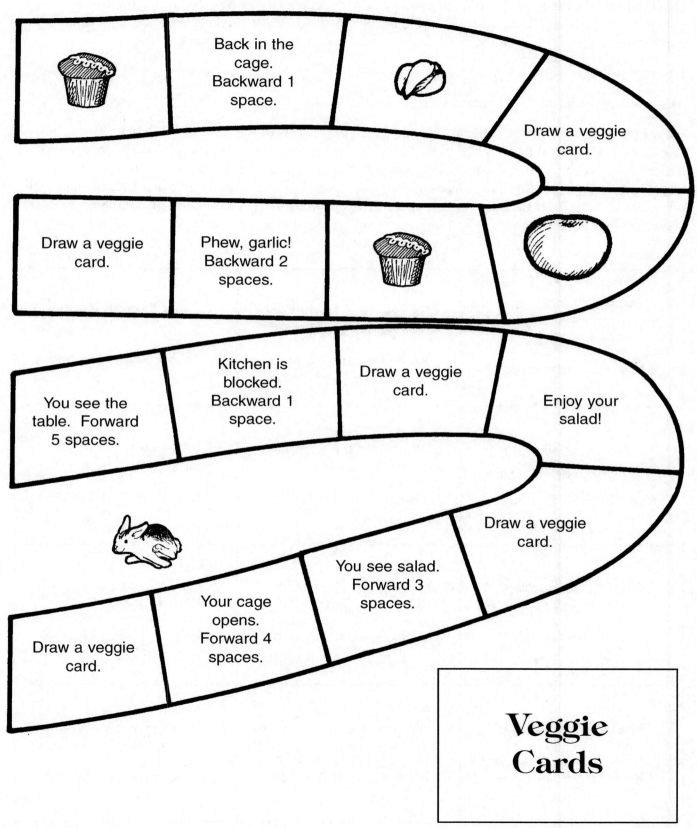

Back in the cage. Backward 1 space.

Draw a veggie card.

Draw a veggie card.

Phew, garlic! Backward 2 spaces.

Kitchen is blocked. Backward 1 space.

Draw a veggie card.

Enjoy your salad!

You see the table. Forward 5 spaces.

Draw a veggie card.

You see salad. Forward 3 spaces.

Your cage opens. Forward 4 spaces.

Draw a veggie card.

Draw a veggie card.

Veggie Cards

Veggie Cards

Directions: Glue the gameboard on pages 24 and 25 together. (It can be glued into a file folder.) Cut out cards on this page on dotted lines and place face down on space marked "Veggie Cards" on the game board.

Number of players: two to four

Materials: gameboard, die, markers, veggie cards

Directions: The object of the game is to see which player gets to the bowl of salad first. Begin by having each player roll the die. The player with the highest roll goes first, rolling the die and moving his or her marker that number of spaces. The player to the left continues the game. If a player lands on a space marked *Veggie Card,* the player to the right chooses a card from the pile and asks the player the question on the card. If the player answers correctly, he or she moves the marker the number of spaces shown on the card. Keep a copy of *Bunnicula* ready for challenges. Good luck!

Name 3 reasons why Chester thought Bunnicula was a vampire. Move forward 1 space.	Explain how Harold got Bunnicula to eat food. Move forward 1 space.	Name 1 way Chester kept Bunnicula from eating. Move forward 1 space.
Who noticed that Bunnicula was starving? Move forward 2 spaces.	Where did the Monroes find Bunnicula? Move forward 1 space.	Name one book mentioned in *Bunnicula.* Move forward 4 spaces.
What made Harold a hero? Move forward 1 space.	Why didn't Chester's steak work? Move forward 2 spaces.	What was Chester's real problem? Move forward 3 spaces.
What are the authors' names? Move forward 1 space.	Who was playing violin music? Move forward 3 spaces.	Who came up with the name "Bunnicula"? Move forward 1 space.

Dining at the Bunny Cafe

Bunnicula has just opened a new restaurant, The Bunny Cafe. The menu is filled with delicious dishes, and Bunnicula could make a fortune. Unfortunately, Bunnicula is not much of a mathematician and has trouble totaling the customers' bills and making change.

Please help Bunnicula become a success! Solve Bunnicula's problems on page 28 by using the menu below.

The Bunny Cafe Menu

Carrot Muffins	2 for $1.00
Spinach Salad	$3.50
Vegetarian Pizza	$3.25
Garden Sandwich	$2.75
Bunny Burger	$2.80
Transylvania Broccoli	$1.20
Bunnicula Beets	75¢
Tomato Juice	50¢
Carrot Juice	75¢
Squash Shake	$1.25
Zucchini Fries	
Small	50¢
Large	90¢
Potato Pie	75¢
Tomato Aspic	60¢

Bunnicula's Problems

Using the menu on page 27, solve these problems on a separate sheet of paper.

1. Toby places an order for two carrot muffins, a Bunny burger, and a squash shake. He pays with a ten dollar bill.

    Order total _____

    Correct change _____

2. Mrs. Monroe orders one carrot muffin, a garden sandwich, and a squash shake. She pays with a five dollar bill.

    Order total _____

    Correct change _____

3. Mr. Monroe decides to order the vegetarian pizza, carrot juice, and tomato aspic. He pays with a five dollar bill.

    Order total _____

    Correct change _____

4. Peter is hungry. He orders two Bunny Burgers, Bunnicula beets, a large order of zucchini fries, potato pie, and a squash shake. He pays for this colossal meal with a twenty dollar bill.

    Order total _____

    Correct change _____

5. Harold is also very hungry because Toby has not fed him chocolate cupcakes recently. He orders three Bunny burgers, two Bunnicula beets, Transylvania broccoli, a large order of zucchini fries, and a squash shake. He pays with a twenty dollar bill.

    Order total _____

    Correct change _____

6. What can you order for $8.00? Choosing items from the menu, try to keep your total as close to $8.00 as you can without going over. Write your work on the back of this paper.

7. Using the menu, write your own problem on the back of this paper and find the answer. Trade problems with a classmate and solve each other's problems.

What Are You Afraid Of?

Everyone has experienced fear of people, places, or things. Sometimes real events occur which scare us, such as a noise outside the house made by a lurking prowler. Sometimes, though, our fears are imagined; for example, a noise outside turns out to be a branch being rubbed against a window by the wind.

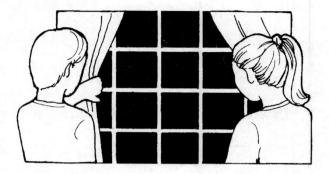

Think of times when you have experienced fear, one real and one imagined. Tell what caused the fear, when it occurred, and how you overcame it.

A Real Fear _____

_____

_____

_____

_____

_____

_____

_____

_____

An Imagined Fear _____

_____

_____

_____

_____

_____

_____

_____

_____

_____

Quiz Time!

Answer the questions for Chapters 7, 8, and 9.

1. Describe what Harold notices about Chester's behavior at the beginning of Chapter 7.

   _____

   _____

2. Describe what Harold notices about Bunnicula's behavior.

   _____

   _____

3. How did Harold discover what was happening to Bunnicula?

   _____

   _____

4. What was Harold's plan to get Bunnicula fed?

   _____

   _____

5. In your own words, what was the "disaster in the dining room"?

   _____

   _____

6. According to the veterinarian, what was Bunnicula's problem and what did he prescribe?

   _____

   _____

7. According to the veterinarian, what was Chester's problem and what did he prescribe?

   _____

   _____

8. Why was Harold relieved after his trip to the veterinarian?

   _____

   _____

9. What changes did Harold observe in Chester's behavior?

   _____

   _____

10. Bunnicula is changed from a scared bunny to a secure family pet. What action does Harold take to show that he is truly accepted?

   _____

   _____

Bunnicula TV Show

A television show can be created by putting together a scroll to wind through a cardboard "television." Divide students into groups of four or five and assign each group a section from the book. Using standard white bond paper, ask each group to illustrate a scene with several drawings, writing a sentence about what is happening beneath the picture. Be sure to have titles and credits. If there is time, they may also wish to add commercials for appropriate products, such as vegetable juice. After all scenes have been drawn, lay them out in correct order and tape them together on the back.

Prepare a TV from a large cardboard carton. Cut a large square for viewing the scroll from the front of the box. Then cut holes in the sides to hold two cardboard rolls, one on top and one on the bottom. The cardboard rolls need to be long enough to extend from the cardboard box so that the scroll can be wound and viewed through the hole cut in the front of the box. (Empty wrapping paper tubes work well.) Leave the box open at the back so that you can insert the scroll when it is ready. You may wish to decorate the front of the box to look like a real TV.

To complete the project, tape the top of the scroll to one tube and the bottom to the second tube, then roll up the scroll so that the title is visible. Insert the tubes into the box and wind the tubes to view. You may wish to allow the groups to take turns watching the show.

Monsters

The vampire, Dracula, is a famous monster. Many other famous monsters have also been created, such as Frankenstein, the Werewolf, and zombies. Each monster has a unique appearance and habits that make it scary to us.

Monsters are said to represent our dark side and our fears. In *Bunnicula*, Chester's jealous feelings cause him to view an innocent bunny as a vampire, and he tries to starve him to death. In fact, in every book or movie about a monster, the creature is killed or made harmless. Unlike the case of Bunnicula, however, we are usually glad to see the monster destroyed.

Working together in a small group, think about monsters that scare or interest you. Then either write about one of these monsters, or invent one of your own. You may use reference books to help you find specific information.

What is the monster's name? _____

Where does it live? _____

What does it look like? _____

How was it created? _____

_____

_____

What power does it have? _____

How does it frighten its victims? _____

How is the monster destroyed, if at all? _____

Researching Bats

In *Bunnicula*, Chester compares the new pet to a vampire bat. Do vampire bats exist? If so, where? What other species of bats can be found? Use an encyclopedia and other resources to research different types of bats.

About Bats

1. In what type of habitat are bats generally found? _____

2. In what geographical regions of the world do bats live? _____

3. How many species of bats exist? _____

4. Because of poor eyesight, bats use *echolocation* to find their way. What is echolocation and how does it work? _____

   _____

   _____

5. Do bats move only through flight, or can they walk? _____

6. What do bats generally eat? _____

7. How do bats reproduce? _____

8. How do bats care for their young? _____

9. What is the scientific name for the bat? _____

10. Write two additional interesting facts you discovered about bats. _____

   _____

About Vampire Bats

1. Where can vampire bats be found? _____

2. What do vampire bats eat? _____

3. What is the scientific name for the vampire bat? _____

4. In your own words, write a paragraph describing the vampire bat and its habits.

   _____

   _____

   _____

   _____

A Family Mystery

The Monroe family had a mystery on their hands: why did their vegetables keep turning white? Fortunately, by the end of the book, the mystery is solved. Has your family ever had a mystery? Maybe someone in your family could not find an important item, or perhaps someone kept eating all the ice cream in the freezer. Whatever it was, it probably seemed like everyone was involved in solving the puzzle of what really happened.

Think of a time when your family had a mystery to solve, then interview each member of your family to get each perspective on what really happened. Write responses from additional family members on the back of this paper.

The mystery: _____

_____

What I believe happened: _____

_____

Family member (_____): _____
                              name

_____

Family member (_____): _____
                              name

_____

Family member (_____): _____
                              name

_____

How the mystery was solved: _____

_____

_____

_____

Any Questions?

When you finished reading *Bunnicula*, did you have some questions that were left unanswered? Write them here.

_____

_____

_____

_____

Then work with a group or by yourself to prepare possible answers for the questions you have asked above or those written below. When you have finished, share your ideas with the class.

- How did Chester become so intelligent?

- How could Harold possibly write a book?

- Why did it take the Monroes so long to notice Bunnicula was starving?

- Why didn't the Monroes give Chester away when he was behaving so strangely?

- Why would a cat be so jealous of a rabbit?

- Why did Toby feed Harold so much junk food?

- What are organic vegetables and what is DDT?

- Is it possible for vegetables to turn white when juice is taken from them?

- What animals have fangs?

- How did Bunnicula open his cage?

- Why didn't Harold take Bunnicula some food?

- Do you think Harold and Chester will become better friends?

- Do you think Bunnicula can talk? How would the book change if he did?

- Do you think the Monroes will ever bring home another stray pet?

- What do you think Chester tells the pet psychiatrist?

- What do you think Bunnicula would tell the pet psychiatrist if he had a chance for a visit? And Harold?

- How could the story have ended differently?

Writing Ideas

Bunnicula can be a springboard for many ideas. The following topics can be assigned for independent story writing, the reading response journals, or for discussion.

- While two siblings fight over a pet snake, it escapes somewhere in the house.

- A real bat flies through an open window and visits a family one night.

- A dog and a cat run away with a gypsy caravan.

- Two detectives find clues that lead them to a monster. But they think it is all a mistake when the monster invites them to tea.

- Two siblings discover the family pet can talk and try to keep it quiet around their parents.

- A cat and a dog have a debate over which is the better pet.

- Family pets fight over who can do the best trick.

- Family pets fight when a human baby comes into the house.

- Something goes terribly wrong in the family vegetable patch.

- The family dog needs shots at the veterinarian and doesn't want to go.

- A terrorized town discovers too late that garlic no longer has any effect on vampires.

- Rewrite a scene from _Bunnicula_ from a point of view other than Harold's.

- Describe the Monroe family house.

- Tell what would happen if you brought home a bunny you discovered during a showing of _Dracula_.

- Think about a pet you know and write what you believe it is thinking during a certain time of day.

- Write a letter from Chester to Harold's editor, telling why the book should not be published.

Book Report Ideas

There are numerous ways to report on a book once you have read it. After you have finished reading *Bunnicula*, choose one method that interests you for reporting on the book. It may be a way that your teacher suggests, an idea of your own, or one of the ways that is mentioned below.

See What I Read?

This report is a visual one. A model of a scene from the story can be created, or a likeness of one or more of the characters from the story can be drawn or sculpted.

Come to Life!

This report is one that lends itself to a group project. A size-appropriate group prepares a scene from the story for dramatization, acts it out, and tells the significance of the scene to the entire class. Costumes and props will add to the dramatization.

A Letter to a Character

In this report, you may write a letter to any character in the story. You may ask him or her any questions that you wish. You may even want to offer some advice on a particular problem.

Guess Who? or What?

This report is similar to Twenty Questions. The reporter gives a series of clues about a character or event in the story in a vague-to-precise, general-to-specific order. After all clues have been given, the character or event must be guessed. After the character has been guessed, the same reporter presents another 20 clues about an event in the story.

Bunnicula Returns!

Write a new story, using Bunnicula as the main character. Other characters from *Bunnicula* may also be used.

Coming Attraction!

Bunnicula is about to be made into a movie, and you have been chosen to design the promotional poster. Include the title and author of the book, a listing of the main characters and the actors who will play them, a drawing of a scene from the book, and a paragraph synopsis of the story.

Book Review

Give an outline of the plot and then your opinion. Be sure to include both positive and negative points.

Literary Interview

This report is done in pairs. One student will pretend to be a character in the story, steeped completely in the persona of his or her character. The other student will play the role of a television or radio interviewer, trying to provide the audience with insights about the character's personality and life. It is the responsibility of the partners to create meaningful questions and appropriate responses.

Research Ideas

Although *Bunnicula* is a fictional story, there are many ideas that bring up questions and suggest topics for further study. Researching and developing a better understanding of such topics enhances one's appreciation of the book and its authors. What topics can you and your classmates suggest?

Work in groups to research one or more of the areas you named above, or the areas that are mentioned below. Share your findings with the rest of the class in any appropriate form of oral presentation.

- Dog breeds
- Cat breeds
- Rabbit breeds
- Organic farming
- Pesticides
- Sibling rivalry
- Psychiatry
- Gypsies
- Vampires
- Veterinary medicine
- Sleeping habits of various animals
- Birth order of siblings
- Romania
- Sherlock Holmes
- Criminal investigation

Pet Diet

In *Bunnicula*, Harold constantly mentions his desire for chocolate cupcakes and other junk foods. Not only is this not a nutritious diet, the fact is that too much chocolate can be poisonous for dogs, while cats, unlike Chester, should not be given milk. Research the following questions to find out more facts about various pet diets. Use an encyclopedia or a pet reference book. Your class may want to invite a veterinarian or a pet shop representative to assist you in this research project.

Questions:

1. What foods are appropriate for each animal?
2. How much should each animal be fed?
3. How often should each animal be fed?
4. What foods should be avoided?
5. What liquids and in what quantity should each animal be given?

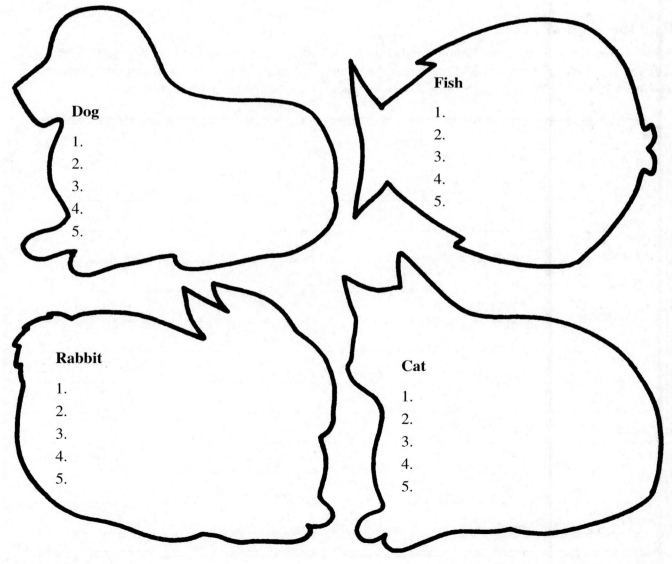

Dog

1.
2.
3.
4.
5.

Fish

1.
2.
3.
4.
5.

Rabbit

1.
2.
3.
4.
5.

Cat

1.
2.
3.
4.
5.

Pet Behavior

Pets are similar in some ways in that they must be taken care of and that they provide enjoyment. Yet, they are also very different in the ways in which they act. Think about a time when you observed cats, dogs, rabbits, and fish. Try to recall how each type of pet behaved. Choose two pets you best remember and answer questions about their behaviors.

1. What activities did each pet enjoy doing?_____

2. What behaviors had each pet been trained to perform, if any?_____

3. What behaviors came naturally to each pet?_____

4. How are these two pets alike? _____

5. How are these two pets different? _____

6. Which type of pet do you prefer? Why? _____

Pet Observation

Scientists gather information about animals by observing their behavior. Carefully observe a pet, either yours or one belonging to a friend, neighbor, or relative. Watch the pet for several minutes and write down what you see, then include your theory, or guess, about why the pet behaved as it did.

Type of pet: _____

Date: _____

Place: _____

Time: _____

Behavior observed: _____

Theory:_____

_____

_____

_____

_____

_____

_____

_____

Unit Test

Matching: Match the quotes with the correct person or animal.

_____ 1. Bunnicula

_____ 2. Harold

_____ 3. Chester

_____ 4. Mrs. Monroe

_____ 5. Mr. Monroe

_____ 6. Toby

_____ 7. Pete

a. "The little guy was shivering from fear and from cold."

b. "Now most people might call me a mongrel but I have some pretty fancy bloodlines running through these veins . . . "

c. "I jumped on a chair, curled up real quick and kept one eye open, pretending to be asleep."

d. "He took this funny-looking white thing out of the refrigerator and held it at arm's length."

e. "Although he's got a rotten sense of humor, he's a nice kid."

f. "I know about this stuff. It's because you buy vegetables that aren't organic."

g. "I'm going to kiss you on your little nose."

True or False

Write true or false next to each statement below.

1._____ Bunnicula was a vampire bunny.

2._____ Harold liked green sourballs.

3._____ Chester did not like his mouse sweater.

4._____ DDT causes vegetables to turn white.

5._____ Toby was reading *Moby Dick* for school.

Short Answer: Provide a short answer for each question.

1. What did Chester say was the reason he wanted to get rid of Bunnicula?_____

2. What was the real reason Chester wanted to get rid of Bunnicula? _____

3. What did Harold notice about Bunnicula that scared him?_____

4. What legend is *Bunnicula* based on?_____

5. What happened to Chester at the end of the book?_____

Essay: Answer these questions on the back of this paper.

1. Describe how Chester came to decide Bunnicula is a vampire bunny.

2. Explain what happened to each of the family pets when they went to the veterinarian.

Responses

Explain the meaning of each of these quotations from *Bunnicula*.

Editor's Note: "We were a typical American family—and still are, though the events related in my story have, of course, had their effect on our lives."

Chapter 1: "'Ma, Toby says he's going to keep the rabbit in his room. That's not fair. Harold sleeps in his room.'"

Chapter 1: "'I wish they had named him Fluffy.'"

Chapter 2: "'What had seemed an ordinary black spot between his ears took on a strange v-shape, which connected with the big black patch that covered his back and each side of his neck.'"

Chapter 3: "'Oh, Chester, I think your reading has gone to your head.'"

Chapter 3: "'But that doesn't mean there's nothing to see.'"

Chapter 3: "'Peter, have you been playing with your chemistry set in here?'"

Chapter 3: "'So it's a white tomato.'"

Chapter 4: "'No, huh? Well, I'd give you one of my cupcakes but I know how much you hate chocolate.'"

Chapter 4: "'It so happens I was discussing great works of literature with Toby.'"

Chapter 4: "'I still don't understand what vampires have to do with our furry little friend.'"

Chapter 5: "'There must be something wrong with our refrigerator. That's it. It's turning all the vegetables white.'"

Chapter 5: "'Hey, Dad, did you leave your brandy glass out last night? Chester is acting a little weird.'"

Chapter 5: "'I tried to warn them, and they wouldn't heed. Now, I'm going to take matters into my own hands.'"

Chapter 6: "'Phew, Chester, what are you wearing that awful thing for? It smells!'"

Chapter 6: "'Doe, Chester, I'be leaving dis roob right dow.'"

Chapter 7: "'I know what you're doing, Chester, and the jig is up.'"

Chapter 7: "'It may seem harsh, but I'm only being cruel to be kind.'"

Chapter 8: "'Mom, doesn't Bunnicula look kinda sick?'"

Chapter 9: "'Case closed, Sherlock?'"

Chapter 9: "'Harold, do you realize we've never communicated? I mean, really communicated?'"

Conversations

Work in groups to write and perform the conversations that might have occurred in the following situations:

- The Monroe family discovers a rabbit in their seats at the movie theater. (4 people)

- Harold and Chester argue about which type of pet is best. (2 people)

- Peter and Toby discuss Chester's strange behavior. (2 people)

- Bunnicula gives Chester a good lecture. (2 people)

- The police are called in by Mr. and Mrs. Monroe to investigate the strange white vegetables. (4 people)

- Toby takes Bunnicula to school for show and tell. (2 people)

- Chester gives a book report on *Bunnicula.* (1 person)

- Harold's editor isn't interested, but Harold convinces him or her to publish the book. (2 people)

- A neighbor complains to Mr. and Mrs. Monroe about the white vegetables in his or her garden. (3 people)

- Chester runs away from home and is returned to Mr. Monroe by police. (4 people)

- Mr. and Mrs. Monroe go to the produce section of the market. (2 people)

- Chester apologizes to Harold. (2 people)

- The veterinarian diagnoses each pet. (4 people)

- Peter feeds the family pets. (4 people)

- Write and perform your own conversation ideas for the class.

Bibliography

Cannon, Janell. *Stellaluna.* (Harcourt Brace and Co., 1993)

Cornish, Louis C. *Transylvania: The Land Beyond the Forest.* (Dorranc, 1947)

Dean, Anabel. *Bats: The Night Fliers.* (Lerner Publications, 1974)

Halton, Cheryl M. *Those Amazing Bats.* (Dillon Press, Inc., 1991)

Howe, James.

> *The Celery Stalks at Midnight.* (Atheneum, 1983)
>
> *Dew Drop Dead: A Sebastian Barth Mystery.* (Atheneum, 1990)
>
> *Eat Your Poison, Dear: A Sebastian Barth Mystery.* (Atheneum, 1986)
>
> *Harold and Chester in Creepy-Crawly Birthday.* (Morrow Junior Books, 1991)
>
> *Harold and Chester in the Fright Before Christmas.* (Morrow Junior Books, 1988)
>
> *Harold and Chester in Scared Silly: A Halloween Treat.* (Morrow Junior Books, 1989)
>
> *Howliday Inn.* (Atheneum, 1982)
>
> *Nighty-Nightmare.* (Atheneum, 1987)
>
> *Rabbit-Cadabra!* (Morrow Junior Books, 1993)
>
> *Return to Howliday Inn.* (Atheneum, Max Macmillan Canada, Max Macmillan International, 1992)
>
> *Stage Fright: A Sebastian Barth Mystery.* (Atheneum, 1986)
>
> *What Eric Knew: A Sebastian Barth Mystery.* (Atheneum, 1985)

Kaufmann, John. *Bats in the Dark.* (Crowell, 1972)

Lauber, Patricia. *Bats: Wings in the Night.* (Random House, 1968)

Lavine, Sigmund A. *Wonders of the Bat World.* (Dodd Mead, 1969)

Leen, Nina. *The Bat.* (Holt, Rinehart, and Winston, 1976)

Naether, Carl A. *The Book of the Domestic Rabbit; Facts and Theories from Many Sources, Including the Author's Own Experience.* (D. McKay Co., 1967)

Schlein, Miriam. *Billions of Bats.* (Lippincott, 1982)

Answer Key

Page 11

1. The Monroes found the bunny at a showing of *Dracula*. Chester imagines that the new pet is a vampire disguised as a rabbit.

2. The bunny has black fur in a cape-like shape, pointed fangs, and slicked back ears.

3. Some possible names were Bun-Bun, Fluffy, Mr. Johnson, Prince, and Dracula.

4. It was a compromise. Bunnicula is Bunny and Dracula combined.

5. Harold is part Russian wolfhound.

6. Chester can talk and speak to Harold. He has a large vocabulary and a vivid imagination.

7. Accept reasonable answers.

8. When Chester heard violin music playing he expected to find a gypsy caravan passing by the house. It turned out to be a neighbor playing his instrument.

9. Chester is afraid the boys will like Bunnicula and ignore him.

10. Accept reasonable answers.

Page 14

1. Transylvania is a region covering central and northwestern Romania. It includes most of Romania's mountains, the Transylvanian plateau, and the northwest plains.

2. The countries adjacent to this region are Hungary, Yugoslavia, Bulgaria, the Ukraine, and Moldova.

3. Transylvania has hot, sunny summers and cold, cloudy winters.

4. The four major geographical regions could include plains, mountains, valleys, a plateau, and rivers.

5. Four natural resources could include iron, lead, lignite, manganese, natural gas, and sulfur.

6. Romanian is the official language.

7. Map of Romania.

8. Accept reasonable answers.

9. Many Romanian peasants believed that vampires existed and the original legend behind the novel took place in this region.

Page 16

1. a. Bunnicula could not move with great energy.

   b. Bunnicula could not play catch.

   c. Bunnicula could not awaken early in the morning.

2. Harold loves chocolate cupcakes and hates green sourballs.

3. Bunnicula leaves his cage and goes to the kitchen.

4. Mr. Monroe finds a white tomato with two holes in it.

5. Chester thinks Bunnicula sucked the juice from the tomato with his fangs.

Answer Key *(cont.)*

6. Bunnicula was found wearing a note written in a rare Carpathian language; he sleeps during the day; he gets in and out of his locked cage; and he has fangs.

7. Accept reasonable answers.

8. They hear the refrigerator click and see Bunnicula running from the kitchen.

9. Harold was the first to investigate the white zucchini.

10. Accept reasonable guesses.

Page 21

1. The Monroe family found a large variety of white vegetables.

2. Pete thought the problem was caused by DDT. He suggested buying organic vegetables.

3. Chester used a towel as a cape and pretended to be a rising corpse.

4. They thought Chester was becoming ill and made him wear a sweater.

5. The sweater was purple and decorated with mice. Chester was embarrassed to be seen in it.

6. The smell was garlic, which is used to ward off vampires. Chester was using it to protect himself from Bunnicula.

7. Mrs. Monroe gave Chester a bath.

8. Harold did not want to harm the rabbit.

9. Stakes, not steaks, are used to kill vampires. Chester is confused about which kind to use.

10. Chester is put outside in the rain, and Harold is glad.

Page 28

1. Total: $5.05

   Change: $4.95

2. Total: $4.50

   Change: $.50

3. Total: $4.60

   Change: $.40

4. Total: $9.25

   Change: $10.75

5. Total: $13.25

   Change: $6.75

6. Answers will vary.

7. Answers will vary.

Page 30

1. Chester was on his very best behavior.

2. Bunnicula was weak and his nose was warm to the touch.

3. Harold caught Chester blocking Bunnicula's way to the kitchen.

4. Harold's plan was to get Bunnicula to the salad bowl.

5. Chester upset the salad bowl, causing Harold to bark; Bunnicula was frightened by Chester and did not get any food.

6. Bunnicula was found to be suffering from extreme hunger and was put on a liquid diet.

7. Chester was diagnosed with a case of sibling rivalry and sent to a pet psychiatrist.

8. Harold found out he did not need shots after all.

9. Chester was in touch with his feelings and wanted to communicate.

10. Harold cuddles Bunnicula and sings him a Carpathian lullaby.

Answer Key *(cont.)*

Page 33

About Bats

1. Bats are found in caves, trees, attics, abandoned buildings, and other dark places.

2. Bats live in temperate and tropical regions.

3. More than 900 species of bats exist.

4. Bats emit a sound which bounces off objects such as insects. The sound bounces back, and the bat uses its keen sense to determine what the object is.

5. Bats can walk but mostly use their feet and legs for hanging upside down.

6. Bats eat insects, scorpions, spiders, fish, lizards, rodents, tree frogs, other bats, plants, nectar, and pollen.

7. Bats are mammals and give birth to live young.

8. Pregnant bats may leave their usual colony and join together in a nursery colony, where they give birth and rear their young.

9. Chiroptera Mammalia Chordata is the scientific name.

10. Accept reasonable answers.

About Vampire Bats

1. Warm regions in the Americas are the homes of vampire bats.

2. Blood is their favorite food.

3. Desmodus Rotundus is the scientific name.

4. Accept reasonable responses.

Page 41–Unit Test, Option 1

Matching

1. a
2. b
3. c
4. g
5. d
6. e
7. f

True or False

1. False
2. False
3. True
4. False
5. False

Short Answer

1. Bunnicula gets milk and Chester does not.
2. jealousy
3. fangs
4. *Dracula*
5. He visits a pet psychiatrist.

Essay

1. Accept reasonable answers.
2. Accept reasonable answers.

Bunnicula Pattern

See page 5 for suggested uses.